WELCOME TO
THE
CHURCH

INTRODUCTION

Promotion? Corporate image? Housestyle? Press relations?! ... Does it sound strange to think of 'marketing' your local church?

Certainly our Christian ancestors were geniuses at 'marketing' their faith in ancient Britain.

Early on, say the sixth century, they developed a 'corporate image' - and stuck to it. Christian churches were instantly recognisable - steeples pointed heavenward to remind people of God. Porches offered shelter - and welcome, with their lovingly carved stonework. The churchyard looked to life beyond death. Walk into any church, and you knew there would be a nave, chancel, vestry, choir, and altar, and what they were there for.

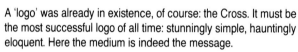

As for the middle management, they invented one of the best known staff uniforms of all time: everyone knows what a monk or nun 'looks like'.

A 'housestyle' was adopted - and rigidly kept. Worship followed the church year - which was the same everywhere. Services, music, the readings, the language ... it all spelled 'Christianity'.

A 'logo' was already in existence, of course: the Cross. It must be the most successful logo of all time: stunningly simple, hauntingly eloquent. Here the medium is indeed the message.

But our Christian forbears did not stop there. In their mission to reach pagan Britain with the Gospel, they used every tool for communication that they had. They made the most of any lay talent and money available to them.

They commissioned their artists to produce large full colour posters - otherwise known as stained glass windows.

Their musicians composed theme tunes - better known as plainsong.

Their editors and graphic artists got busy in the publications department:- and produced magnificent illuminated Bibles and manuscripts.

Their painters and stonemasons used visual aids to retell the old Bible stories: via thousands of statues and wall paintings.

Others had only cheerful enthusiasm and a good sense of timing - so they went on to invent religious broadcasting - by ringing the church bells.

Of course it sounds incongruous to refer to early Christian witness in the language of modern public relations. But there is no denying that these Christians 'presented' themselves brilliantly by simply following the golden rules of effective communication, which have not changed in 14 centuries:

- They knew what their message was, and could sum it up clearly and simply.

- They knew exactly who they wanted to reach.

- They used methods of communication that made sense to the people of that time.

2

This was a Public Relations dream come true. No wonder that small, poor groups of Christians surrounded by large, indifferent, and often hostile pagan communities managed to catch their attention, earn their respect, convert them - and change the course of British history.

Of course, that was on a national level, over centuries. But it was only achieved by the witness of thousands of individual churches using whatever talents and opportunities they had.

So what about today? Does the image your church presents to the local community make sense to the people of our time? Whether you want to have an 'image' or not, you still have one. An image is simply how other people perceive you.

The message you intend may not be the message you are sending, which would be a great shame, because in this age of the media, image counts more than ever.

Nowadays we have developed a defence mechanism to cope with the thousands of images that we see every day of our lives. If we like something we see, we ask more questions. If it doesn't immediately attract us, we filter it out, and are distracted by something else.

This is a handbook with ideas on how to make the most of your church - in promoting Christianity.

The ideas are simple and need not be expensive.

They don't take an inordinate amount of time and PR expertise.

Above all, they are not intended to transform you into something you may not be - a 'trendy' church. The ideas are simply to help you to make the most of what you are.

They are TOOLS to help you communicate. With them your church can become more effective, both in talking to itself, and in gaining the interest of the community.

So where do you start? At the beginning - where you are.

Where are you? Find out with an audit of your present communications.

Section 1 DO A CHURCH AUDIT

A simple audit can be done with four questions:

- How does your church communicate now?
- Who are the people your church is aiming at?
- What does your church say is its message?
- What are the local people seeing and hearing?

HOW DOES YOUR CHURCH COMMUNICATE?

Gather together in one place everything it produces, both for members and for the community.

This might include:

- Headed notepaper of the parish
- Pewsheets
- Church magazine
- Leaflets on your church history or church events
- Stewardship envelopes
- Posters
- Welcome packs
- Church calendars/diaries

Examine everything critically. Does it look as though it all came from the same organisation? Or is it in different typefaces, styles of layout and colour?

Make a list of all the other ways in which your church communicates.

This might include:
- Church noticeboard
- Display board in church porch
- Display board at back of church/church bookstall

Are your display boards in good condition? Are they painted roughly to the same colour scheme? Are the typefaces used on the different boards reasonably similar?

Ideally, all your forms of communication will work together, and not against each other.

WHO ARE THE PEOPLE YOUR CHURCH IS AIMING AT?

Move out into the neighbourhood.

a) Buy a local map and trace your church's catchment area.

b) Mark out the schools, shops, hospitals, train stations, pubs, libraries, leisure centres, council estates, old people's homes, roads of privately-owned houses.

c) What sort of people live in the area? Where do they work? Do they commute? Where do they spend their leisure time? What is the ethnic mix? Is any age range or family grouping more prominent than others? How long do they tend to stay in the area?

4

Talk to local people who work in the community: doctors, teachers, health visitors, counsellors, librarians. They can give you guidance on your neighbours' lifestyles, on widespread problems.

Ask newsagents which newspapers sell best: those with columns of sober print or those with many photographs and short captions. Ask your video shop: which videos are most popular? Ask your librarian: what sort of books are most borrowed?

Draw up a profile of the people which your church should be aiming to reach. Undoubtedly, you will find they break down into several sub-groups, from ethnic communities to the retired.

WHAT DOES YOUR CHURCH SAY IS ITS MESSAGE?

Ask your congregation how they think the church is seen by the community. You might take five minutes in a service to ask them to fill in a simple questionnaire.

Include questions asking: What are we best at? Where do we need improvement? Do strangers find us friendly? Is our tiny tots group well known and used, or a profound secret? What sort of adjectives would the congregation like to use to describe their ideal church? Formal or informal? Organ and choir or guitars? Mission based or holding the (crumbling) fort?

WHAT ARE THE LOCAL PEOPLE SEEING AND HEARING?

Finally – and this is the tricky bit – you need to ask the local people about the church. A good way is to position some polite volunteers near local shops with a list of questions that will take two minutes only. Tell them not to mention your particular church immediately.

Your questions might run like this:
- Are you local?
- Have you attended any local churches?
- If so, why? Marriage? Funeral? Other?
- Have you heard of *(your church)*? If so,
- How did you hear of it?
- Which following words would you use to describe it? *(eg: Welcoming • Modern • Old-fashioned Out of touch • Lively • Sincere • Any others?)*
- Which of its activities have you heard of?
- Thank the person politely, no matter what they've told you!

Interview about 40 people.

Analyse the responses – they will help you pinpoint where action is needed. For example – if they've heard of all the local churches except yours, you've got a major job ahead! If they knew your church was there, but didn't realise it had midweek activities, that's another challenge, etc.

Now you have got a better idea of your community, and who you are aiming to reach.

You have also got a better idea of how they see your church. Do you recognise it as the place you know and love?

It will be of great advantage to your church to adopt a design style and use it on all its printed materials: magazine, letter headed paper, noticeboard, pewsheets, etc. Logos in particular are invaluable shortcuts to help people recognise your church quickly, easily and with confidence.

LOGOS - KEEP THEM SIMPLE

A logo is usually the name of the organisation set in a specific typeface and colour, and accompanied (sometimes) by unique graphics.

A great deal of thought and money can be spent by companies on getting the 'mix' right, because every one of those ingredients can project a different image.

Certainly typefaces are packed with personality. Compare The Times with The Daily Mirror. Or TEXAS with Harrods. The typefaces reflect the nature of the companies. There will be one to suit your church's character. Your local printer will have a large selection and can guide you.

Colour, too, can influence the way you perceive a company. Would you eat at Pizza Hut if their signs were grey?

As for graphics, think of the nobility and stamina implicit in Lloyds Bank's racing Black Horse. Suppose Lloyds used instead a running rabbit? Look at your church's name, location, and history. Anything there to inspire an artist to create a symbol evocative of your church? For instance, a church called St Francis might include a robin perched on one of the letters in Francis.

Deciding on a logo for your church need not be expensive, but it will almost certainly be traumatic, as you will get as many different opinions as people involved!

Essentially, a good logo is:

- simple in design

- easily recognisable

- can be used in a wide range of settings, from posters to bookmarks, from stationery to newspaper adverts.

At the very least, your church can simply decide that it will use a particular typeface and mix of upper/lower case to write its name. Any printer could construct such a logo for you which you could then incorporate in your printed material.

I AM DELIGHTED TO PRESENT A DESIGN THAT INCLUDES EVERY SINGLE ONE OF THE COMMITTEE'S IDEAS!

CHOOSING A TYPEFACE

Again, try and match your typeface to the character of your parish. If you have guitars and overhead projectors at your main Sunday worship service, Gothic lettering outside on the noticeboard would mislead people. Similarly, if you have Sung Mattins, breezy typefaces would not make this clear.

If your printer knows what sort of message you want your church to be sending out, he/she can advise you on typefaces to choose from.

Some examples:

Zapf Chancery is quite an old-fashioned, formal face, most used for invitations, headlines, noticeboards, etc – but it is not easily readable when used in large amounts of body text.
Numbers: 1 2 3 4 5 6 7 8 9 0

Times (a serif face) is one of the most popular typefaces of all time for a good reason — it is easily readable and looks good in body copy. Projects a conservative, middle-of-the-road image. Goes well as body copy with Helvetica (see below) headlines, or vice-versa.
Numbers: 1 2 3 4 5 6 7 8 9 0

Century, another good serif typeface, slightly more stylised than Times.
Numbers: 1 2 3 4 5 6 7 8 9 0

Helvetica, the most popular sans-serif typeface. Always looks clean and modern, without being too "way-out". Goes well with Times (see above). Works well as headline or body copy face - this booklet uses Helvetica Condensed for body text.
Numbers: 1 2 3 4 5 6 7 8 9 0

Avant Garde, as the name implies, is a modern face much favoured by "with-it" designers, etc. Actually, not the best choice for body text, but good for projecting a more up-beat image.
Numbers: 1 2 3 4 5 6 7 8 9 0

Dominante is the typeface chosen for the headlines in this booklet. It is quite a fashionable face, but best used in small doses.
Numbers: 1 2 3 4 5 6 7 8 9 0

BALLOON, IN CONTRAST, IS REALLY A POSTER FACE — IT ONLY COMES IN CAPITALS, BUT IT IS AN INFORMAL, FRIENDLY HEADLINE FACE.
NUMBERS: 1 2 3 4 5 6 7 8 9 0

Formal Script: I have included an example of this, if only to implore you to use it as little as possible. It is difficult to read and is only useful to give a very old-fashioned flavour to a small amount of copy.
Numbers: 1 2 3 4 5 6 7 8 9 0

CHOOSING A COLOUR

It is no mystery why MacDonalds uses orange in its interiors: psychologists say that orange reduces self-restraint and encourages impulsive action: like buying a Big Mac. So whatever colours your parish uses, it is sending out subtle messages.

For example:

RED   is up-beat, assertive, exciting. Use it to grab attention. But beware, too much of it can overwhelm and increase tension – avoid if dealing with overtired or over-stressed people.

BLUE   is peaceful, trustworthy, constant, orderly. Use it in mid tones to project confidence. But beware if you are launching an exciting, creative new parish scheme.

BROWN   is homely, gregarious. Use it when you want people to open up their hearts to you. It is the least threatening of colours; investigative journalists wear it. But beware, people don't rally or march to brown.

YELLOW/ORANGE   is cheerful, uninhibited, sociable. Use it with children. Yellow is their favourite colour. Use it also for fun events – it cheers you up and encourages frivolous, irresponsible behaviour. But beware, it is not suitable for anything serious.

GREEN   is nurturing and dependable. Use it when people are over-stressed. But beware, fund raisers have found that people avoid them most when they wear green.

So what colour best suits your church, its interior decoration and its noticeboard? Think through the main message you want to get across, and choose accordingly.

Just a tip: according to one expert, a bright mid-tone blue with white lettering works wonders on church noticeboards.

Once you've got a housestyle (or should that be churchstyle?), stick with the format. Use it every chance you get.

Let's begin outside your church, with the church noticeboard . . .

Your church has a prime advertising site - its own noticeboard. It advertises your church 24 hours a day, seven days a week. And your church noticeboard may be much more. It may be one of the very few remaining points of contact between Christianity and much of your local community.

So if it uses too many strange ecclesiastical words like 'surrogate', or 'solemnisation' or uses jargon like 'come and see the Holy Spirit move mightily', it will only confirm in non-Christian minds that this church is totally unrelated to daily life - certainly *their* daily life - and will only welcome people who also speak this strange language.

If your board is also in poor shape, with paintwork peeling, it will suggest to passersby that the Christians are about to shut up shop and move out as well.

The impact of your church noticeboard can't be overestimated. So make it work hard, and well, for you.

This is even more vital if you have to lock your church during the week.

Here are some ideas for revamping your church noticeboard:

1. You just can't beat original research. Why not ask a photography enthusiast in your congregation to spend a day with a friend touring the area and photographing as many church noticeboards as possible?

2. You need the friend to go along because you will want them to help measure the size of each of the noticeboards, and roughly how far back from the road/trees they stand.

3. You are now in an excellent position to hold a 'potluck' supper at somebody's house and watch the slideshow of church noticeboards. Tell people from other churches about it and they will be so impressed that they might want to come along and see - and even be willing to pay a small entry fee - which could offset your costs.

4. The slides will soon break down into three groups: the attractive noticeboards, the indifferent noticeboards and the really awful noticeboards.

5. Save the slides that really attract the group and analyse why they do so. With this in mind, you can consider what you might do with your board.

What are your options?

1. POSITION IN THE CHURCHYARD

Take into account lines of vision. Is the board clear to people directly in front? Approaching from either side? In cars? On the other side of the road?

Ask some volunteers to walk/drive by your church. Where do they say is most convenient and eye-catching?

2. SIZE OF BOARD

Don't be shy. While you are at it, you may as well make it worth doing. Five feet wide and two and a half feet deep should give you enough space.

3. PLAN AHEAD CAREFULLY

It would be best if someone skilled at painting actually painted the sign for you. Tell him/her the size of the letters you want and ask him/her to tell you:

- the amount of lines possible on the board size you have chosen

- how many characters (letters – not church personalities) a line? That is how much copy you are going to get on there. That much and no more. There are many grey areas in life, but with character counts it really is a matter of black and white … So it's best to have this at the back of your mind before you start composing a sign that will wow the neighbourhood and stop the traffic.

4. CONTENT

So what might go up on this sign? Well, how often are you prepared to change it? Bear this in mind when you think what information should be included. The name of your church is an obvious beginning. Then also of course, the minister, and details of your Sunday services and midweek activities. It welcomes people to come along to them.

Specific details such as times and names are bound to change as the years go by. But if you don't include some of them, your sign could stand forever and say nothing.

For instance, do you include your minister's name? It certainly adds a personal dimension to the church.

If you decide to go ahead, how will you refer to him – or her?

Research has shown that the use of Christian names gives a warm, human feel, especially to strangers who have to contact them for major personal events such as baptisms, weddings or funerals.

There is also a strong argument for listing the whole range of activities of your church. How else will people know of your mothers and toddlers groups, young wives, men's breakfast clubs, young people, Sunday schools, house groups and prayer circles?

If these groups are subject to frequent change, how about: "For times and venues of our wide range of activities that serve the community and to which you are welcome, please see details in the church porch or local library."

In an ideal world, your noticeboard will also have a clever little display box with perspex into which you can slip posters announcing Christmas carols, coffee mornings, missions, etc. (Please don't leave Christmas carol notices up until Easter!)

You may, though, have to settle for a line that says: For details of church officers and current activities, please consult notices in church porch . . .

PLEASE don't use posters covered in cling film or a freezer bag: they look so utterly forlorn. Why not have one laminated by your local printer instead?

5.   IT'S NOT WHAT YOU SAY, IT'S THE WAY THAT YOU SAY IT

You are talking to the general public, not just members of your own denomination. Keep your wording simple and jargon free. Ask friends who are not Christians to read your draft and see how much it would mean to them.

6.   COLOUR AND CONSTRUCTION

The board itself needs to be bright and sympathetic. Black is formal, stand-offish and unsympathetic. Deep ruby red, bright medium blue, or rich emerald green are excellent choices. What about lettering? Gold on ruby, gold or white on blue, gold or white on green are all excellent choices. One expert swears that white on motorway sign blue works wonders.

Finally, is it weatherproof? Today's varnishes should make certain. Rotting wood and peeling paint never inspired anyone.

Assume the local youths will consider your sign an unfinished masterpiece . . . and want to add their own contributions. Ask the local police, if no one else can help you, how you might discourage their artistic leanings. Graffiti proof materials are available – at a price.

With grateful acknowledgement to the Rev Robert Ellis, Communications Officer in the Lichfield Diocese for the work he has done on the effectiveness of Church noticeboards.

This is a true story: there is a church whose porch is utterly empty except for a huge, luridly coloured poster from the police which says sternly: Lock Your Cars. Thieves About.

What does this convey to casual visitors to the church?

1. The members of this congregation are a secret gang of car thieves. You have been warned.

2. This parish is an island surrounded by a community of car thieves who will pinch your car the minute you come in here to sing a hymn.

What it does *not* convey is many things that that church may well be: a friendly, warm, supportive community that welcomes newcomers, and has a faith which it celebrates.

So some tips on how to make the most of your church porch:

- Appoint someone to keep it clean. Breezes blow in a fantastic amount of grit and stray bits of paper.

- Consider putting up some sort of large noticeboard with information aimed at both members of the congregation and the general public. This is especially helpful if you have had to keep information on your churchboard outside to a minimum.

You might include:

BACK TO BASICS

Names and numbers of the ministry team, church officers etc, and where they can be contacted. Details of all regular church activities, plus names of the group leaders and how to contact them, plus venues and times of meetings.

Details of what to do if people want to use the church for a baptism, wedding or funeral.

Details of when confirmation classes are held.

Details of when the priest is available for confession or counselling.

CHURCH PORCH Section 4

POSTERS

A poster with a challenging or encouraging thought. There are superb Christian full colour posters on the market which are cheerful and enlivening, and easily available from your Christian bookshop.

EMERGENCY

Consider that non-Christians sometimes drift into churches at times of crisis in their lives. Don't leave them hammering on the door of a locked church. It will seem to them that God has forsaken them too. Instead, in a prominent place in your porch, why not give details of what people in great personal need can do to get emergency help? Repeat here that the minister will see them, or at least give the number of the local Samaritans.

THE KEY TO IT ALL

If you must keep your church locked, give the details of where visitors can obtain the key. Would a nearby trustworthy shop be willing to act as a contact point, and ring you to let you know you have visitors? Or what about a rota of people who take it in turn to let any visitors in?

SAY IT WITH FLOWERS

Other churches make their porches welcoming by adding vases of dried flowers, or posters commissioned from children and young people in the congregation.

How hard a display section at the back of your church has to work will depend on how much information you were able to give out on the church porch.

So - basic essentials if you have not given them out in the porch:

- name(s) of clergy and where reached

- names of relevant church officers and where reached

- times of services

- details of regular church activities - group leaders, times and venues of meetings

- details of how to ask for weddings, baptisms, funerals

- details of confirmation and other classes (for Lent, etc.)

But there is a great deal more to be made of a display section at the back of your church. Whether it is simply a table, or a display board over a bookcase, or a freestanding screen, you might want to consider including some of the following:

- A one page introduction to your church's history

- A one page introduction to your church today - introduce your priest or minister, church officers, and group leaders, etc. Some churches include photographs of these key people

- A 'post box' area where letters for people in the church can be left

- Details of any current church campaigns

- Details of any current diocesan/district campaigns

- News from missionary or other national church societies

- Posters done by the Sunday Club

- Accept 'advertising' from members of the church (sale of household items, offers of lifts to town, babysitting, etc.) In student areas - details of Christians offering lodging. In retired areas - details of help needed/offered.

- A church calendar for 'Coming This Week' - and list everything happening in the church diary that week. (Make sure it is changed every Sunday!)

- Details from your Cycles of Prayer

- Anonymous prayer requests - written on specially provided slips of paper

- Details of any support ministries offered: one church has a group of ladies who run a group called 'Casseroles for the bereaved'. Could you offer such a service? How about 'Lifts for people visiting families in hospital' or 'Casseroles for families in crisis'?

As for design, why not think of having your display board in your church colour? With the name/logo at the top?

Make sure that everything that goes up is printed in the housestyle of the church.

The church bookstall is your church's window on the wider Church. Through it you have access to inspiring stories of Christians around the world, to Church history, to explanations of the Christian faith, and to practical Christian advice in dealing with life's problems.

It can enrich your church's life immeasurably.

It can provide invaluable back-up to preparation for baptism, and confirmations. It can help people prepare for their marriages, and come to terms with their bereavements.

So, if you decide to have a bookstall, be assured the effort is well worth it; there is minimal cost involved, and there are several easy ways to go about it.

Begin by contacting a Christian bookshop near you. They are the ones who will supply you with whatever stock you choose.

HOW LARGE A BOOKSTALL?

First you have to decide how large a bookstall you want. It could be:

1. A small selection of Bible Reading Notes, and greeting cards laid out at the back of the church after the service each week. Expense is minimal, and you operate on sale or return.

WHEN YOU'VE PUT DOWN YOUR "BOOK BARGAINS OF THE WEEK" THEN I'LL BEGIN MY SERMON!!

2. **A £100 Bookstall:** Invest in £100 worth of books from your bookshop, and keep them in stock in your church for a month. At the end of that month, go back to your bookshop. Exchange all your books for a new selection of books, and use any money you've got from sale of books to buy

more books to make it back up to the £100. Do this each month, and your church will have a constant selection of new books from which to choose. Your bookshop should give you a 10% discount, which means that, in time, you will be able to earn back your original £100 investment, and then the project becomes self-financing, and even makes a tiny profit.

The only problem with such bookstalls is that if the bookshop is supplying many of them in the area, it means that a large selection of its stock is on display only one day a week, as opposed to six days. This will hurt the bookshop's turnover.

3. **A Special Events Bookstall:** This is an excellent alternative for meeting the needs of both churches and bookshops. You arrange with your Christian bookshop that for several major events in the church's year (for example, Patronal Festival, Confirmation, Harvest Supper and Christmas Fete), you would like to have several hundred pounds worth of stock for one day only.

If you book it up well ahead of time, the bookshop can supply you with a wide selection of books and Christian music and posters and what-have-you. Anything that is not sold is returned.

WHAT BOOKS TO CHOOSE

Choosing stock will, of course, be a joint effort between you and the bookshop manager. If you tell them a bit about what sort of people come to your church, they will know what sort of readership to cater for. Bookshop managers can also supply you with copies of publishers' catalogues, which you can borrow to browse through to your heart's content.

You can match stock to major events in the church's year. Offer Lent Books to read. Preparing for Confirmations. What is Christmas all about?

Consider the sort of problems people in your congregation face. There are books of Christian teaching on handling your money, managing your time, raising your children, getting along with your spouse, dealing with unemployment, and coping with depression, to mention but a few.

WHAT ELSE TO OFFER

You might consider adding a music section to your bookstall. There is a good deal of traditional and modern available today on CD or cassette.

You can also have customised tea towels, mugs, keyrings, calendars and postcards produced featuring your church. A number of companies offer this service - your Christian bookshop will advise you.

CHURCH LIBRARY

There may be dozens of Christian books floating around your congregation. Why not marshall them together, and have people give them to you on loan for a few months as part of a church library?

BOOKSTALLS Section 6

These could be offered to the housebound, elderly or ill people who may not want to spend out on books. They can also be offered to new Christians.

If you bought in a stock of books on Preparing For Baptism, Marriage, etc, the minister could lend them to people preparing for these major events.

In any event, Christian publishing houses can offer you a vast amount of literature to enrich and build up the spiritual life of your church. It really is worthwhile taking advantage of this splendid resource.

LEGAL NICETIES

In order to get a discount from your Christian bookshop, you need a licence from the Publishers' Association. Contact them at 19 Bedford Square, London WC1B 3HJ (0171 580 6321).

In the unlikely event that you damage the stock of Christian books in your care, make sure your insurance covers it. The bookshop will probably not accept liability.

BOOK AGENTS' LICENCES - A RESALE SCHEME

The Church Book Agency, and its variants are for the *resale* of Religious Books only, and the books obtained cannot be used in a Church Library, or given as Sunday School prizes, or be prescribed or recommended reading for teaching or training purposes.

Books are obtained from a Bookshop whose name and address is endorsed on the Licence and who is in consequence enabled to give the Book Agency a discount which otherwise, under the Terms and Conditions of The Net Book Agreement 1957, would not be permissible on Net priced books.

The Licence is issued on a once-only payment (apart from requested amendments), without annual renewal, but it is not transferable from person to person, or from organisation to organisation.

The Licence may carry a maximum of three Bookshop suppliers at any one time. Any later additions to make up this number or changes must be submitted to The Publishers Association on the appropriate amendment form, together with the licence and the current fee.

Acceptance of Responsibility must be undertaken by an official of the organisation, ie a Minister of Religion, or the Vicar or Priest in charge of a Church, on a form provided and which usually accompanies the Licence application form. The undertaking is considered binding upon their successors.

It is a condition of granting such a Licence that it may be revoked at any time by The Publishers Association upon reason being given and upon its giving written notice by hand of its secretary to the parties named thereon. But, unless revoked on account of any action which The Publishers Association considers to be a breach of its terms and/or conditions, three months' notice shall be given to the Licensee.

Welcome packs probably began in the United States and they are becoming popular over here now too.

WHAT IS IT?

A booklet or series of sheets introducing people outside the church to the weekly life of the church, its people and activities.

WHY BOTHER?

Because no matter how stunning your church noticeboard is, people can't keep it in the drawer for easy reference.

Because you can pack so much more information on to paper than on to signs.

Because it is an excellent tool for non-threatening outreach by your church.

WHO IS IT AIMED AT?

- people new to your church catchment area
- people new to your church

WHERE YOU DISTRIBUTE IT

- obviously, to anyone who visits your church and who looks as though they might come back.
- but also, why not leave several at your local library, church schools (for the families of new pupils), estate agents, doctors' surgeries, and tourist information.

WHAT IT COULD CONTAIN

Depending on where you were going to distribute it, you might want to include:

A section on community information:
- a paragraph on the area itself – historical interest, main industries, special landmarks, etc.
- handy phone numbers: town council, hospitals, libraries, tourist information, schools, places of interest, lists of surgeries, vets, dentists, local refuse tip.

A section on your church in its wider context
- who are the other nearest churches to you
- how many churches in the area
- how many of your denomination
- what diocese/administrative area you are within and address and phone number
- who your bishop/chairman/moderator is.

A section on your church, in particular

- when built

- how it got its name

- brief resume of its history/ any historical highlights

- brief details of anything of architectural interest

- the clergy: where they're from, how long at the church, names of spouses and children. Their hopes for the church; any particular hobbies, etc.

- make up of current congregation: size, families/singles/students/retired/children

- a typical year in the life of your church – calendar highlights

- a section each on the groups in your church, from Mothers and Toddlers to Youth Groups

- introduce the various leaders of the church, such as choirmaster, churchwardens, etc.

WHAT IT COULD LOOK LIKE

- A4 or A5 sheets stapled together or put into A3 folded to A4 folder

- At its simplest, a series of A4 sheets with church logo at the top that can be run off at will, each one containing a separate section of information. Then you can add or subtract information relevant to the readership. (Whether giving it out via estate agents or at the door of your own church to someone who has lived in the vicinity for years.)

ADVERTISING?

Why not?

Contact your local companies and tradesmen and explain your project. Tell them you are compiling a sheet that will contain advertisements, and that you promise to always include this in every pack given out.

If you are careful to use only reputable firms, newcomers to the area will find this very valuable as they search for painters, decorators, plumbers, solicitors . . .

Here's a really easy, failsafe and fairly cheap way of helping the church to communicate with itself. A weekly news-sheet is a single sheet of A4 paper folded lengthways or sideways. The sidesmen and women hand them out to worshippers each Sunday morning along with their hymn books and prayer books.

ITS PURPOSE

To give details of the worship service and events in the coming week at church.

CONTENTS MIGHT INCLUDE

READ ALL ABOUT IT..!!

- service details
- which hymns to be sung
- Bible readings with brief introduction
- special prayers
- introducing baptism/banns of marriage
- prayer requests
- special events happening that week
- theme of the week
- activities for that week's church diary
- other notices that the minister wants to give out.

PRODUCTION POSSIBILITIES

- if you have a well equipped church office – no problem!
- If someone in the congregation owns a word processor or better still, a Desk Top Publishing (DTP) programme, and is willing to type it each week, you are home and dry.
- Ask a local printer what he'd charge you to photocopy however many copies you need each week in exchange for an acknowledgement of this in the news-sheet.

DESIGN

- With DTP facilities a really professional looking job can be done.
- But don't despair if all you have is a typewriter. Begin by having a banner heading for your newsheet created by a local printer. Then type your weekly version on to copies of this, and photocopy the results.
- If at all possible, use your church logo, colour, and housestyle in typesetting.

LEAFLETS Section 9

Never underestimate the power of a leaflet!

They can help you publicise a wide range of events and activities, are generally cheap to produce (especially if you have someone in the congregation with a word processor), can be targeted very closely to the readership, and easily passed from person to person.

Use them for:
- introducing your church
- publicising an event
- welcoming newcomers to your church or area
- introducing your Christian faith to the community
- explaining a point of view - ie from Sunday trading to the occult.

Here are 4 key questions to ask yourself before producing a leaflet:

WHY ARE YOU PRODUCING IT?

Try and answer in one sentence: eg "To give special information about the outside service in June".

If you have too many reasons for one leaflet, you are probably trying to put too much into it! Consider producing separate leaflets.

Once you have a single focus for the leaflet, you will find it easier to make sure everything works towards this one purpose.

WHO ARE YOU HOPING WILL READ IT?

Identify your target audience as closely as you can.

Then put yourself in their place, and read the leaflet, asking yourself: How would I react to receiving this? Study other magazines and literature that specialise for this audience.

WHAT INFORMATION DO WE INCLUDE?

This should be fairly straightforward - say what you have to say.
- Avoid complicated language and religious jargon
- Be clear about the action you want the reader to take. For example, 'phone for more details' 'pray for . . .', 'call . . .', 'come along . . .' Give phone numbers and names.

HOW SHOULD THE LEAFLET LOOK?

Any five people will probably give you five different answers. It is probably best to give the final decision to one person, and accept that you cannot please everyone.

Design and Format: Aim to make your leaflets and brochures look as professional as possible. Collect all the leaflets on anything you can get your hands on. Go to the local library and town hall - they usually have many on offer, free. Pay special attention to the leaflets that drop through your letterbox. Your church will be competing with these. Keep a file of them - it will become your ideas file for layout. Spending a few extra pounds on quality paper or printing may make all the difference in getting your leaflets read or thrown away. And that would be a real waste of money!

21

FINAL THINGS TO ASK YOURSELF

1. **COMMUNICATE POLITELY:** Use words and images the readers understand and enjoy.

2. **ALWAYS TRY AND REDUCE THE NUMBER OF WORDS:** The more to the point you are, the better.

3. **SIZE OF LEAFLET:** Most are based on the common A4 size (210mm x 297mm). Sheets can be folded into 'gatefold', or three, to give a leaflet that opens either horizontally or vertically. A4 size sheets can also be folded in half to A5 size (148mm x 210mm) although this generally is best kept for single sheet handbills. If you stray outside standard paper sizes your printing costs will soar.

4. **TYPE OF PAPER OR CARD:** A standard cartridge paper will usually do (80 gram bond) but you may want to invest in a thin card or better quality paper for a leaflet that is designated to be kept for a longer period. Any printer will have a wide selection for you to compare the weights.

   Coloured paper will give your leaflets more appeal, with black and white or another colour lettering printed on a strong colour. Take care with tinted papers – some convey a cheap, weak effect.

   Consider using recycled paper to demonstrate your church is caring for God's world, and add a note saying you have done so.

5. **QUANTITY:** After all the work you've put into your leaflet, you will be tempted to have thousands printed. Resist this. Calculate carefully and realistically how many you will need, and then add 10 per cent for unexpected demand.

6. **DISTRIBUTION:** Should be planned carefully. Methods include:

   - handed to passers-by
   - dropped through letterboxes
   - delivered with one of the local free newspapers
   - given to people visited by church members
   - given to visitors to the church
   - left at local information centres and libraries.

Work out the most effective way of using the leaflet and get them into use as quickly as possible. There is something very depressing about finding a pile of well produced leaflets gathering dust in a corner of the church foyer.

Leaflets used properly can help your church by storing information in an easy to transmit way. But they can only reinforce people to people contact – they can never replace it. Your church should never use leaflets in order to avoid contacting people face to face.

Posters remind your neighbourhood that your church is alive and active and wanting to involve the local community. Posters are excellent at publishing your church activities.

If you design them well, and use messages that have an appeal in your neighbourhood, you will create goodwill towards the church.

Do you have any artists in your church? Could this be a lay ministry for them?

SIZE AND COLOUR

An excellent size for a poster is 508mm (20 inches) wide by 762mm (30 inches) deep – sometimes still known as 'double crown'. Next best is the A2 size (420mm x 594mm). Both sizes will be available from your local printers.

If your budget is very limited, again, look for someone with a graphics software package on their word processor. It can produce excellent A4 sized posters.

Remember the power of colour! Bright and cheerful. If it is a fun event (Fayre on village green), go for yellow or orange. If an event on peaceful lines (Seminar on how to deal with stress in your life) in green. If a rally (church in local mission - come and hear . . .) why not use red?

The main thing is to make sure the lettering stands out loud and clear from the background of the poster.

I HOPE YOU DON'T MIND...
BUT MY GRANDAUGHTER HELPED
ME WITH THIS POSTER......!!

HOUSESTYLE AND TYPEFACE

It is vital that you include your church's logo/housestyle on the posters – so people will know at a glance where the poster 'comes from'.

If the poster has to be done by hand, Letraset is one alternative. Or neat and clear freehand lettering – but be sure it IS neat and clear!

Poster paints are very effective - and great fun to use!

LAYOUT

You can let your artistic tendencies go wild. For a Christmas poster, why not lay out the lines in a shape of a tree?

Don't be afraid of blank space. It enhances the visual impact of the words.

CONTENT

- keep the 'title' brief
- list the information in order of its importance
- include:
  the what, when, where, why and how much, plus a phone number for more information. Try to start with an eye-catching phrase: *(see right)*

CONCERT FOR BOSNIA

✦✦✦

African Children's Choir sing for Bosnia

at

St Mary's Dingle

at 7.30 pm

on

Saturday 20th August

✦✦✦

All proceeds in aid of the Bosnian Refugees

✦✦✦

Tickets: £5.00
For details ring: 606060

WHERE DO YOU PUT A POSTER?

This depends on your budget. If you can afford large posters that are waterproof, ask at the town hall for space on local billboards. Bus companies also offer advertising. This sort of space would probably best suit a really major church event, or local event involving several churches.

Some councils give local voluntary groups a low rate for poster boards.

Otherwise, you might use posters printed on normal cartridge weight paper and pin them up in the following places:

Newsagents, library, doctors' surgeries, tourist office, bus stops, town hall, village hall, social welfare offices, church school bulletin boards, village post office, local newpaper offices (where they might be so interested they'll do a story on you! More of this later . . .)

Finally:

- keep a record of what was used and when
- change your posters regularly – especially after the event advertised has taken place!

A NATIONAL CIRCULATION OF MILLIONS

Never has so much been produced by so few with so little for so many. There's no doubt about it – church magazine editors and their teams are the unsung heroes of our time. Despite little manpower and money they have a circulation of millions throughout the country.

But who reads them? Ah well, that depends on the quality of the particular church magazine in question. If it is badly produced, with dense, tedious copy of little interest to the reader, the magazine probably goes straight in the bin. If, on the other hand, the magazine is clear, well presented, and has relevant, easy-to-read material, then it may well read. There is still a widespread friendliness to local churches, and many people are willing to give you a chance.

So this section is devoted to helping you make the most of this chance.

Let's begin at the beginning: your church is a Christian community. It has a busy life of its own, as well as a Christian presence to maintain in the wider community. It needs some sort of regular vehicle of communication with its actual and potential membership.

Think of the magazine as a conversation you are holding with members of the church and also with anyone interested out in the wider community. In conversation with people, you don't think up a number of subjects and simply hold forth ad nauseum (think of those bores who do!). Hopefully you find out a bit about the person to whom you are speaking, and then adjust your conversation accordingly. You seek for common ground, and build on it.

It is the same when you consider your readership – if the subjects you think of tackling in your magazine aren't worth telling them in conversation, will they really want to read about it?

Which leads us on to this vital question. Who do you think your readers are? Just church people, or also some of the wider community? Who would you like them to be?

The majority of the editorial decisions you make about your magazine will depend on who you are trying to reach.

Go through your magazine and list the items you think would be of interest to just church people, to people on the fringe, and to both at the same time. This will help you decide if your current magazine fulfils the role you have in mind for it.

Better yet, hold an anonymous, simple survey of the magazine's contents amongst some of its present readers.

Get them to go through copies of the past three issues of the magazine and put a '1' beside those items of great interest, a '2' beside items of medium interest, a '3' beside items they didn't bother to read, and a '4' beside items they thought a total waste of space.

Whatever the results, don't let your feelings be too hurt. Bear in mind some hard facts of life:- most of your readers are undoubtedly far less committed than you would like them to be to the affairs of the church.

So be kind to yourselves. Accept that a 'target' readership of both people in the church and people in your area is trying to span a chasm that would defeat even national periodicals. It is hard to imagine how a special interest magazine aimed at dedicated members of a church community can also be successfully aimed at people who just happen to live within the church's catchment area. It's like saying car magazines should be written for both car enthusiasts *and* those who live near petrol stations. This is not to say that people in your catchment area won't be interested in the magazine, but to them it will be more an eavesdropping exercise than direct participation.

On the positive side of things, a well-edited church magazine can provide a great deal:

- a regular expression of the Christian presence and witness to the neighbourhood
- a reflection of the social life of the Christian community
- a timetable of events at the church (plus the times and venues)
- rotas of various duties

So what does a well-edited and well-produced church magazine look like? It is hard to set specifics. Churches, their manpower and financial resources vary so widely from area to area that it is impossible to say that any one type of publication is right for everyone.

If you would like to give your church magazine a fitness test, here is a checklist of things to consider.

1. FREQUENCY OF PUBLICATION

This can be:
- Weekly
- Fortnightly
- Monthly
- Bi-monthly
- Occasionally

If your church publishes a weekly news-sheet of coming events, then a magazine could concentrate on the wider church life, and need not come out so often.

2. LENGTH

Anything from 2 sides to a vast number is produced. If you do run to many pages, make sure that each page counts for something and is really necessary. Less is often more. It is better to produce six pages well than 12 pages badly.

IDEAS FOR A5 PAGE LAYOUTS

An A4 sheet folding in half and printing on both sides to give a 4 page newsletter.

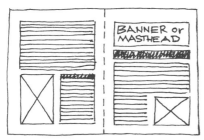

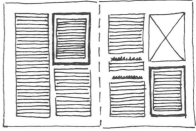

A VERY STRAIGHTFORWARD SINGLE COLUMN LAYOUT. FULL PAGE WIDTH OR HALF WHEN PICTURES ARE INSERTED.

A DOUBLE COLUMN LAYOUT USING BOXED PANELS FOR FEATURES. TYPE IN BOXES NEEDS TO BE TO A NARROWER MEASURE.

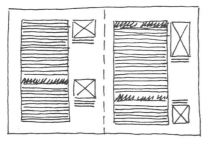

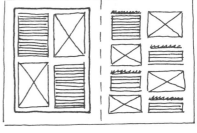

A WIDE SINGLE COLUMN WITH PICTURES IN THE "MARGIN." THIS REQUIRES A LOT OF WHITE SPACE BUT LOOKS VERY NEAT.

A DOUBLE COLUMN LAYOUT USING PICTURES AND TEXT SYMMETRICALY GIVES A VERY TIDY APPEARANCE.

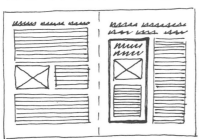

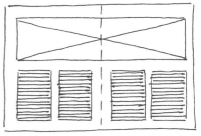

A MIXTURE OF LAYOUTS, FEATURING SINGLE AND DOUBLE COLUMNS. THIS ALLOWS EACH ARTICLE TO HAVE ITS OWN FLAVOUR.

A LAYOUT ONLY REALLY USEFUL WHEN YOU HAVE PANORAMIC STYLE PICTURES OR LARGE GROUPED PHOTOGRAPHS.

IDEAS FOR A4 PAGE LAYOUTS

Usually a single unfolded sheet printing on one or both sides.

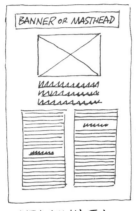
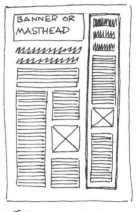

THREE COLUMN GRID GIVES YOU GREATER FLEXIBILITY THAN A5 GRIDS. SINGLE OR DOUBLE SIDED.

WHEN YOU HAVE A STRONG PICTURE AND PLENTY OF SPACE, THIS 2 COLUMN LAYOUT WORKS WELL

THREE COLUMN LAYOUT AS A 'FRONT' OR 'COVER', WITH A SINGLE FEATURE COLUMN.

ALTHOUGH A3 IS RATHER LARGE, THE LAYOUT POSSIBILITIES ARE ALMOST INFINITE. YOU CAN USE THE BEST OF A5 AND A4. THE SKETCH HERE SHOWS WHAT COULD BE DONE ALTHOUGH AVOID THIS UNLESS YOU ARE VERY CONFIDENT. AND HAVE FLEXIBLE COPY AND PICTURES.

3. SIZE

This can be A5, A4, or tabloid newspaper for the really ambitious!

Many printers say that A5 is user-friendly in these sort of publications, as they don't flop as much as the A4 size. On the other hand, there is much more scope for exciting layouts and artwork on an A4 format.

4. PRODUCTION

(i) *Preparing the copy:*

- Typewriter
- Word processor
- Desktop publishing package

TYPEWRITER:

If you are stuck with a typewriter, don't despair, just make sure . . .

a) That all the contents of the magazine are typed on the same machine. Nothing looks worse than a hotchpotch of typewriter faces!

b) That the ribbon is as black as you can make it. Grey typing leads to grey copies.

c) That you do not fill each page with print. This will look very dull. Don't be afraid of white space and wide margins. Consider Letraset for your headlines, and instant art for some illustrations.

WORD PROCESSOR:

Basically, this is just a computerised typewriter; but with most word processing packages you will have a much wider range of typefaces and typesizes – and the ability to print in bold and italic. Most word processors come with a dot matrix printer: as with typewriters, make sure you have a good black ribbon and the quality will be acceptable. If you can output to a laser printer, you will get a much better quality original from which to print.

DESKTOP PUBLISHING PACKAGING:

Much more sophisticated than word processing, enabling you to create graphics, put text at an angle, put in background tints, etc, and make up complete pages before output. You can output to dot matrix, but this will restrict what you can do – a laser printer is almost essential. Perhaps someone in your church has access to one?

(ii) *Printing the copy:*

THE WAX STENCIL DUPLICATOR:

For runs up to 600. Reliable, economical. But the paper is absorbent, and images can normally only be typed directly on to the stencil. Not recommended for many typewriters.

OFFSET LITHO:

Runs up to several thousands. A true printing press, excellent results. Any paper, any colour. Second hand bargains for sale. But requires some skill to operate it, and takes time to set up.

THE PHOTOCOPIER:

Runs up to several hundred. Clean, excellent copies. Better quality than duplicator, more convenient than litho. But copiers are prone to go wrong. Lease, rather than buy, from a firm offering swift repair service.

THE PROFESSIONAL PRINTER:

Obviously the best, but expensive.

5. READERSHIP

Can vary from simply the church's members to a group of churches, an ecumenical association, and the wider community.

6. TONE

You are the local Christian presence – and the tone of the magazine should reflect your faith and witness.

7. PRICE

- The readers pay by annual subscription or a price per copy. This may lose you some intended readers who are unwilling to pay.

- The readers pay, subsidised by advertisements. Can work well, but can also keep prices artificially low.

- The readers pay, subsidised by church funds. But this can conceal inefficiency and again, keep the price artificially low.

- The advertisers pay, but you must guarantee them a large enough circulation – usually house to house delivery. Ask enough, but not too much. Many tradespeople will advertise with you as a gesture of goodwill, and you want to keep theirs.

  Handy tip: Remember that back covers are more valuable than inside pages.

Many churches pre-print ads for a year ahead. They do a set of between 12 and 16 display adverts on two sides of a single 'through' sheet of paper. This becomes four pages when it is collated into the finished magazine. Simple display adverts can often be made by adapting a sample of the advertiser's letterheading or business card.

Make sure your editorial copy is easily distinguishable from the ads. Use a different typeface, a ruled box, or a different colour paper.

Whatever adverts you have, make sure the advertisers receive a complimentary copy of the finished publication.

8. EDITORIAL TEAM

Whether it is a one-man enterprise (shame on you – it is too big a burden for one person) or a large, well-organised team with reporters, an advertisement manager, and layout artist, there are certain qualities to look for in the editor:

- an ability to put forth ideas in a simple way
- an eye for details
- a feel for what interests people
- assurance in dealing with the printed word
- some flair for writing and presentation

An editor's job breaks down into five roles:

a) Commissioning the right kind of material. Look out for things happening in the church's life, and get reports. Recognising when important issues are being debated and making sure readers have the Christian perspective.

b) Pruning material sent in (often quite severely). This takes judgment, firmness and tact – because contributors complain.

c) Balancing the material. Charles Lane, founder of the Church News Service, put it this way: Every church magazine should contain:
- **GOSPEL** – items to do with the church's teaching and worship;
- **ACTS** – stories of things happening in the life of the church;
- **EPISTLES** – comment and reflection linking faith and daily living; and
- **REVELATION** – wit and wisdom to illuminate all the rest.

b) Planning the look of the pages to make the most of the relative news value of the different items appearing.

c) Setting the tone of the publication. Ensuring the style and content convey a feeling of credibility to the readers. Making sure the magazine does not read like the social doings of a local leisure club, but of a spirit-filled Christian community.

9. TITLE

Surprisingly, not all magazines have one. At least, give the full name and address of your church somewhere inside!

For names, you could choose some alliterations: eg St Mark's Messenger; St Gabriel's Good News; Twywell Tidings. Or take a theme from your church's name. St Botolph is the patron saint of wayfarers. Call it The Wayfarer. For a St Peter's, why not The Fisherman? or Cross Keys? For St Francis, why not The Pilgrim? And so on.

10. COVER

Pre-printed covers in full colour are printed by the publishers Mowbrays and the Bible Lands Society . . .

Or use local art students to design you line drawings of your church, etc, and print in different colours for use throughout the year.

Or forget a front cover; get your artist to design a masthead – a distinctive motif with the title of the publication, the church, and the address, which need fill only a small space at the top. Then put your major story on the front page.

11. CONTENT

A sensible menu would include at least some of the following:

- name and **full** postal address of church and clergy (surprising how many forget this!)

- an expression of Christian faith, presence and witness (Bible study material; topics for prayer)

- An expression of the social life of the Christian community (news of people and church groups)

- a timetable of church events; times, dates and venues plus reports of the church council

- rotas of special duties

- message from the clergy – but not necessarily as the first item!

- puzzles and crosswords (as teaching aids)

- news of the wider church, including syndicated material supplied ready for printing

12. WRITING TO BE READ

Somerset Maugham wrote: *'To write simply is as difficult as to be good'.* You are already good, of course, so writing simply should not be too difficult:

a) Try to keep sentences to about 15 words long. Divide longer ones.

b) Avoid subordinate clauses at the beginning of a sentence.

> For example:
>
> *NOT*   'Even though one might be tempted to fall asleep during sermons, staying awake is more polite.'
>
> *BUT*   'It may be tempting to sleep during sermons, but staying awake is more polite.'

c) Use short words in place of long ones whenever possible.

> For example:
>
> *NOT*   'commence', 'observe', 'consider'
>
> *BUT*   'begin', 'see', 'think'

d) Use one word in place of two or more whenever possible.

For example:

NOT   'We made our way . . .'

BUT   'We went . . .'

e) Be ruthless in cutting out 'thinking time' phrases. These are distracting in print.

For example: 'It seems to me . . . What we often fail to realise . . . It is good to report that . . .'

f) Try and turn all abstract nouns into verbs.

For example:

NOT   'There is pressure on the Church Council to withhold Quota payments.'

BUT   'Some people are pressing Church Council members to refuse to pay this year's Quota.'

g) Make all verbs active. You then have to say who did it. Try applying this rule to the church council minutes!

For example:

NOT   'Coffee will be served.'

BUT   'Members of the youth group will serve coffee.'

h) Use the spoken word in short memorable quotations to describe feelings or opinions of the speaker.

j) Keep paragraphs short – 60 words or less, made up of four or five sentences. The shorter the better.

k) Limit what you write to 300–400 words at most. Your piece will then fill about one and a half pages of a typical small format magazine. Most people will skip reading anything longer anyway.

13. THE WAY TO SLANT A STORY FOR YOUR MAGAZINE

a) Make it personal. Tell your story as news about people rather than organisations.

Name names. Thus:

NOT   'The Sunday School outing was well attended with many enjoying a picnic in the park.'

BUT   'Mary Smith shared the last sausage with the vicar under the oak tree at last Saturday's Sunday School outing . . .' and then go on to give more details of the outing.

b) Make it local. If you cannot give a subject a local slant, it does not belong in your local church magazine. Thus, tackle child slavery in Brazil via news of a local organisation who is fighting it.

c) Make it topical - but beware the time-lag between writing and publication.

d) Make it relevant. If people are concerned about the Church Commissioners' financial losses, report on how it will affect your church.

14. THE WAY TO WRITE A STORY FOR YOUR MAGAZINE

Remember what Rudyard Kipling said:

> 'I have six honest serving men;
> they've taught me all I know.
> Their names are Who? and What? and When?
> and Where? and Why? and How?

If you can work these six honest serving men into your story in the right order, you will be well on your way.

The most powerful force in Britain today is the media. It is a multi-billion pound industry which creates our very culture by shaping the lives and opinions of millions.

Yet what we've got now is small beer compared to what's coming: by the year 2000 there will be at least 40 TV channels and 400 radio stations.

Radio is fast and cheap; and there's a lot of it about. More likely than not, it's Local Radio with which you will have most contact - either BBC Local Radio or Independent Local Radio (commercial radio). The BBC now provides 38 local radio services in England on a broadly county-wide basis. More than 100 services are provided by independent local radio. In terms of popularity, local radio (BBC & ILR) is certainly the most listened to.

BBC local radio tends to have much more talk and therefore a little more time for your contribution. Because the audience can't see you, what you say and how you say it is important. You need to sound friendly, firm and talk conversationally in easily understood phrases. Independent local radio is dominated by music. If you're given an opportunity to say something, be prepared to be lively, brief and to the point. This is where the 'sound bite' comes in - a simple, short statement of the most important thing you want to say, delivered in a colourful manner!

WHERE DOES THE CHURCH FIT IN TO ALL THIS?

As far as the media is concerned:

The Church, locally and nationally, is an important part of the community. Therefore it is of interest to the media, who will listen when it speaks on matters social, moral, ethical, political, royal, and in times of crisis or disaster.

Section 12   GAINING MEDIA ATTENTION

As far as the Church is concerned:

It is vitally important that the Church does speak publicly on these matters. Sociologists warn that most religious practice has already become dangerously 'privatised' - restricted to people's spare time, but not allowed to interfere with the 'real world'.

This is exactly the opposite of how Christianity began life.

Christ told his disciples they were to be the light of the world, the salt of the earth, a city set on a hill, witnessing to his coming, death and Resurrection. They obeyed him - and took their Faith into the marketplace.

Think of the media as the 20th century equivalent to the marketplace: full of noise, distractions, conflicting interests, full of sceptics, full of critics, and everyone trying to sell you something.

Christianity belongs here. Our faith is meant to be communicated to a world in need, not kept to ourselves.

WHERE DOES YOUR CHURCH FIT IN?

Of course, the mere mention of the word 'media' is enough to strike fear into the hearts of people who have had unpleasant brushes with it in the past. But the media are not going to go away, and if you handle them correctly, it is possible to have a creative and beneficial relationship with your local newspaper, or radio and TV station.

WHAT IS NEWS?

The media are interested in news. What is news?

News is about the major events that shape society. It is about change ... what is exceptional, what is different. It is primarily about people . . . the famous, the powerful, the influential, the victim, the accused. It is about matters that affect society either materially, emotionally or physically.

News is about:

- **SOMETHING NEW**
  If it is already common knowledge, then it's not news. *"Cathedral facelift continues"* is not news. *"Blind stonemason repairs Cathedral"* is.

- **SOMEBODY EXTRAORDINARY DOING SOMETHING ORDINARY**
  "Jill Jones opens Church Fayre" is not news.
  "Princess Diana donates fitness cycle to charity auction" is.

- **SOMEBODY ORDINARY DOING SOMETHING EXTRAORDINARY**
  "Jill Jones sings solo at Carol Service" is not news.
  "Jill Jones clears church yard with bulldozer" is.

- **SOMETHING TOPICAL**

  "Bishop of Warmouth resigned last week" is not news.

  "Bishop of Warmouth announces resignation" is . . . especially if it's unexpected.

- **SOMETHING DIFFERENT**

  "Vicar holds garden party for roof appeal" is not news.

  "Vicar parachutes to roof appeal party" is.

- **SOMETHING LOCAL**

  "Dutch missionary arrested in Brazil" is not local news.

  "Local Vicar arrested in Moscow" is.

- **SOMETHING SOMEONE IS TRYING TO KEEP SECRET**

  As one newspaper proprietor said, "News is what somebody somewhere wants to suppress; all the rest is advertising!"

GAINING MEDIA ATTENTION

Gaining media attention is the most cost effective means
of promotion your church can undertake.
So how do you go about it?

- **Have a hit list**

  Compile a mailing list of all the media outlets in your area: newspapers, radio and TV, local or regional news agencies and free sheets. Most libraries keep lists or try Benns Media Directory or Willings Press Guide in the reference library.

- **Keep your eyes and ears open**

  Read your local papers. Get to know their style. Note each section: news, features, finance, sport, motoring, women, etc.

  Listen to your local radio station and watch regional TV programmes – and think how you might get coverage.

  Get to know who's who at the newsdesk or newsroom. Keep your list up to date. Cultivate a personal contact.

  Learn the deadlines and plan with these in mind.

WRITING A NEWS/PRESS RELEASE

Newspapers, radio and TV stations are inundated with news releases. Most end up in the dustbin. To make sure yours doesn't, present one that catches the journalists' attention, and which they can use to give your church the publicity it wants.

HOW TO WRITE A NEWS/PRESS RELEASE

Gather all the facts and make sure you know what your story line is. Then ask: "What is the target audience for this story? ... people in the pew, other churches, people generally, politicians, opinion formers? Which medium will best reach this target audience? ... radio, television, press, local or national, church press, all of them, some of them?"

To draw attention to your story some key words and phrases might well help! The oldest ... Biggest .. Highest ... Smallest ... For the first time ever ... Great concern ... Urgent appeal ... Controversial ... For the last time ... Crisis ... Serious ... Object to ...

Make sure your News Release is well laid out. Keep it short and to the point. Lead with the main fact of statement and present it in the most interesting way. Give your story punch without distorting the truth of what you're saying. Use simple language and short paragraphs. Don't use jargon; theological or "in" phrases.

WHAT TO DO

- A release should read like a news story, not a letter or a report. A news story demands five facts: WHO? WHAT? WHERE? WHEN? WHY?

- The first paragraph is vital. Its impact decides whether the reader will continue with the rest of your story. A useful tip is that as many of the "five Ws" as possible should be included in that first paragraph.

- Interest created with the introduction must be retained throughout the story. So use your imagination as you develop the facts. These must be placed in descending order of importance as the news release will be cut from the bottom up.

- The second paragraph should draw out the implications of your opening statement. The third paragraph should then contain detailed information - facts and figures.

- Subsequent paragraphs can then expand on the information and comment on the implications.

- Use a quote. This makes the story come alive by expressing personality or strong opinion.

- Choose a simple headline that sums up the main point of the story.

- Type your release neatly using double line spacing with a wide margin either side to allow the sub-editor to make notes. At the bottom of the last paragraph type "ENDS".

- Use standard A4 paper. Make sure the name of the church or organisation is clearly printed at the top of the first page and that, at the end, you give a contact name and telephone number(s), (office and/or home).

- Type at the top, in large bold letters, "NEWS RELEASE", date it and indicate when the information can be published - "For immediate use". Use an embargo* only when really necessary. The words "Embargoed until (time and date)" should then be typed at the top of all pages. *(* an embargo is an instruction not to publish before a specified time and date.)*

- Try to keep your news release on one page: two pages should only be an occasional breaking of the rules. If you have a lot to say, get the main points into the news release and spell out the whole story in a longer information sheet to go with it. News editors receive hundreds of news releases every week. If yours is not to end up in the wastepaper bin, keep it short.

- Offer photos or photo opportunities - a picture is worth a thousand words! The print media are always after good photos; if there is action involved, television too.

- Address your news release to the News Editor unless you are sending it to a particular journalist or reporter. If you are, make sure you spell his or her name correctly. Keep a copy of everything you send.

When you have sent your news release be prepared for a phone call or a visit from a reporter - so be available. Think out what further information you are willing to disclose. Follow up with a phone call if they fail to contact you.

Media outlets are not there for your free advertising, so don't use a News Release for an ordinary event. Instead, send details to the "WHAT'S ON DIARY". For a News Release there must be a news angle which must be factual and not based on hearsay.

It takes only a little imagination to develop a few basic facts into an interesting story; and you will improve with practice. Even if they don't use it, at least they know you exist. They know you're bright and imaginative and the church may not be dead after all. Your news release says things about your church and your faith as well as about your story - so make sure it's good. If it is used it might not be recognisable when it finally appears. If it comes out just as you wrote it - you're getting good!

HERE IS A GOOD EXAMPLE OF A NEWS RELEASE

The Parish Church of St. Peter

Parish Office, Hayle Street, Tutshill, Birmingham, BR8 3TF
Telephone 021 743 9785

News Release

18 December 1992   **FOR IMMEDIATE USE**

VICAR IN CARDBOARD BOX RAISES MONEY FOR HOMELESS

The Revd George Johnson will swap his bed for a cardboard box throughout January
to raise money for the homeless.

Mr Johnson, 46, hopes his 31 nights in a cardboard box outside St. Peter's Church,
Tutshill, where he is Vicar, will draw attention to Birmingham's homeless people.

This vigil will begin at 8.00pm on Friday 1st January 1992 when Mr Johnson
climbs into his box with a copy of the Bible and a candle.

Through his efforts he hopes to raise at least £4,000 towards Birmingham's target
of £500,000 pounds for the Churches Homes for the Homeless (CHH).

CHH, launched by Churches Together in Birmingham in June 1990, supports practical housing
projects throughout the city.

Mr Johnson said: "My discomfort will end on 31st January. I can only hope that the
£4,000 we raise will go a small way towards the Churches Homes for the Homeless
goal of providing shelter for those who have no other choice but to sleep on the streets".

ENDS

For further information contact:
Mr Johnson, telephone, 021 743 9785 or
Mrs Celia Barker, telephone, 021 743 8430

WHEN A REPORTER CALLS

- Introduction

    The print and electronic media work fast. If you can catch their attention, they'll be on to you immediately. So most inquiries to you will come in the form of an unexpected phone call (unless you've sent out a news release!).

    As a result, it is easy to be caught off guard and to make comments before you have got your mind into gear. A simple routine procedure, whatever time of day (or night) the call is received, reduces the risk of the hasty remark.

    Reporters come in three types – long standing, experienced and new. You are safest with the experienced reporter. They've been around, know enough to understand most of what you say, and are intent on getting a good story. Long-standing reporters may well "know" what you are going to say before you say it, so make sure they are listening to you! They may also know what they want you to say, so watch out for leading questions. New reporters, though they might know little about the story, will be intent on making their own reputation, so beware. Be prepared to spend time carefully explaining the background.

WHAT TO DO

- If the telephone call is unexpected, find out what they want and ask them to ring back in five minutes. This gives you time to think, and write out briefly what you want to say. If you agree to ring back, make sure you do! Always be courteous; rude people make bad news.

- If a busy reporter suggests visiting you, welcome this and make sure the kettle is on. If the request is for a radio or television interview see "The Radio or Television Interview" for additional advice.

- It is always best in giving information to the media to be factual, frank, deliberate and to the point – but always in a firm, friendly manner.

- Answer questions in your own words and in complete sentences - a "yes" or "no" to a loaded question can have startling consequences!

- You're not bound to answer every question - don't be bullied. If possible make sure that you control the interview - in an astute and gentle way.

- Be positive – mere denials or "no comment" suggests you have something to hide. It could be an opportunity to kill false rumours. Mistakes multiply when people refuse to talk, so be helpful and the reporter will usually respond in the same way.

- If you have problems answering a question, don't flannel. If appropriate, tell the reporter you'll find out and call back.

- The reporter has column inches/air minutes to fill. Feed him/her your facts in a way that dictates the angle of the interview. If you don't want it reported – don't say it!

- Rarely, if ever, go "off the record". It just isn't worth it or safe. This is not to misjudge the reporter. Rather, if something is worth saying, be honest and say it.

- Never try to pull rank on a reporter – unless you happen to be the majority shareholder on his board of directors!

- If further advice or help is needed, contact your Diocesan Communications Officer or District Press Officer.

- In matters with wider implications, even if you have answered the query, still tell your Diocesan Communications Officer or District Press Officer.

A "YES" OR "NO" TO A LOADED QUESTION CAN HAVE STARTLING CONSEQUENCES!

UNDERSTANDING THE MEDIUM

Broadcasting is the most fleeting of communication media. If you are asked to appear on radio or television bear in mind:

- Broadcasting is there to entertain, to inform, to educate. Your aim is to offer your listeners or viewers something interesting to think about. Prepare to paint pictures with your words, give examples, and relate what you say to everyday life.

- Attention must be gained immediately, and kept. Don't waffle: the listener or viewer can switch off or change channels.

- Information must be presented clearly: people can re-read newspaper articles; they cannot re-listen to radio or TV.

- Your voice and appearance will play an important part in getting your message across: radio and TV tend to leave people with very strong impressions. You'll have heard the phrase "The image is the message". Unfortunate but true.

CONVERSATIONS WITH AN AIM

In essence, an 'interview' on radio or television is a conversation with an aim. When you are invited to be interviewed, you are the person with the information – the specialist, if you like. The interviewer asks for that information, seeks further explanation, then, where relevant, wants you to justify what you are saying.

Listeners are, in effect, eavesdropping on the conversation. They can then form their own judgments about the validity of the points being made.

THE INTERVIEWER: DEVIL INCARNATE OR DEVIL'S ADVOCATE?

Interviewers are rarely "out to get you" for the sake of it. When they play devil's advocate, their purpose is not to create confrontation, but to achieve a better interview. The harder questions provoke sharper answers, e.g. "Why did you decide to adopt this policy?" is better than "Tell me about your new policy".

Interviewers are not experts but they are experts at appearing to be experts. You will always know more about your subject than the interviewer.

HOW TO GO ABOUT IT

- Most requests for an interview are made by phone. Before agreeing, find out some basic information. Ask for details of the programme and find out what they want to know and why.

- They will ask – WHO?, WHAT?, WHERE?, WHEN?, and HOW? – the kinds of questions the listener or viewer would want to ask.

- Time is important. Find out when and where they will want you, how long it will last, and whether the interview will be 'live' or pre-recorded. If it is 'live', before you begin find out what the first question will be.

- Prepare by writing down the main points you want to get across - maximum of three points plus supporting arguments. Check relevant facts, be sure of what you want to say and practice with a colleague or friend.

- Being interviewed is a one to one conversation with the interviewer; but remember that an audience will be listening - eavesdropping! Find out what you can about the audience - the chances are they will not be specialists in your subject, even if they are interested. Target your preparation accordingly.

- What you look like and the general impression you create have much more impact on most people than anything you say. Look good, even for radio and especially for television! If possible, know something about the interviewer and be sure they know who you are.

- Listen carefully to the questions and illustrate your answers with examples and anecdotes. Concentrate on the interviewer's face, make eye contact, try to look relaxed and smile. Do not rush in to fill natural silence.

- Don't be intimidated. You will usually know far more about the topic than the person asking the questions. The interviewer's only role is to draw you out, to help you tell your story. You are the expert but be prepared for the occasional personal question.

- Adopt a conversational and lively style, keep it brief, simple and avoid jargon. Cutting in is unattractive but, if you decide it is necessary, do it decisively or don't do it at all.

- Use the opportunity for maximum benefit. Whatever questions are asked be sure to say what you want to say. Use the subject of the questions to make the points you want to make. Never get angry . . . there could be a next time!

- In a television interview ignore the camera, look at the interviewer and speak directly to him or her.

- If the reporter visits you, go somewhere quiet - a small room or inside a car is good. Ignore the microphone - it will be held about 12″ away from you.

- When they first call for a telephone interview, always ask them to phone back in five minutes. Use that time to make notes - your three points. Do not write a script, you will sound wooden.

- In a studio interview, do not thump the table or rustle papers. If you need to take notes with you have them clearly written on small cards.

PUT YOUR CHURCH IN THE PICTURE

Newspapers are insatiably hungry for attention-grabbing photographs. Why not feed them? A good photo can 'make' an indifferent story.

Next time you plan a church event, plan to tempt the picture editor of your local newspaper into sending along a photographer.

Remember that what seems way over the top in real life is probably just about right for a news photograph. Excellent bait includes:

- Minister in cassock and apron helping to cook at summer fete or flipping pancakes for Shrove Tuesday.
- Choir singing while slowly roller skating in procession through town, wearing placards to advertise coming church event.
- Local celebrities releasing hundreds of balloons outside church to launch appeal.
- Visiting church dignitary digging some turf, sitting on a motorcycle, milking a cow (and if he can manage this all at the same time, you'll attract ITN's News at Ten!)

....DON'T CARE HOW BIG
THE FIRE AT THE OIL REFINERY IS—
WANT YOUR TOP PHOTOGRAPHER
HERE; AND I WANT HIM NOW!!

PLANNING A PHOTOCALL

If you want to lead a harrassed life, become a newspaper photographer. They work to tight deadlines under ceaseless pressure. So keep the following points in focus to guarantee the best exposure from them:

- Ask yourself exactly what message you want to get across, and how it can best be REPRESENTED VISUALLY. The more material you can offer a photographer who arrives with, say 20 minutes to 'do' your church, to work with, the better.

- The SUBJECT must be photogenic. You need an appeal launched, a building opened: don't be satisfied with a short speech from the vicar. Add the release of a hundred balloons or a dozen doves. Or why not get members of the Junior Church to stage a mock tug-of-war until the ribbon breaks?

- The BACKGROUND must be visually interesting, if at all possible. The inside of a modern church hall rarely falls into this category. You want to launch a mission: why not get the congregation to meet outside at the start of the service and all light a candle and sing a hymn? Mention in your press release that Jesus called his followers the 'light of the world . . .'

- Have some PROPS available. Consider using children (dressed as Bible characters?), unusual objects, over-sized cheques, balloons, doves (at Pentecost), donkeys (on Palm Sunday), sheep (at Christmas). You are launching a Mothers and Toddlers group: why shouldn't the minister push a pram - followed by all the mothers and toddlers and babies - around the block?

- When you send a news/ press release to the Picture Editor only, remember to write at the top "ATTENTION PICTURE EDITOR" - and describe your event from the visual point of view.

- Remember that the News Desks and Picture Desks are separate, and that you can't expect journalists to communicate with each other! So whenever you write a news release on a story with any visual aspect, at least send a copy of it with a brief note to the Picture Desk as well.

AT THE PHOTOCALL

- Accept that the photographer will fuss about, close curtains, move chairs, clear desks, button jackets, smooth hair. They are after the best lighting and the least clutter.

- But don't be manipulated. A TV company once begged a Dean to flood his Cathedral – and make it a temporary ice skating rink for some story or other. The Dean politely declined, but did the decent thing: offered an alternative. He invited a small flock of sheep to visit the cathedral and be shown around by a Border collie. The press sadly hung up their skates but followed the dog following the sheep. In the end a good time was had by all – though the photographs came out a bit woolly!

- Encourage the subject to be co-operative, to relax and smile. A frowning, tight-lipped Guides' leader is not a pretty sight.

WHAT IF THE PROMISED PHOTOGRAPHER NEVER DEVELOPS?

- Don't grizzle – you are competing with sudden explosions, bank robberies, and car crashes. Or maybe the 'job' listed before yours that day is taking longer than foreseen – speeches overrun, mayors are delayed.

- Instead, have as a back-up, a parish press photographer who can take photographs for you. Many newspapers today can handle colour film, but supply them with prints at least 5″ x 7″. If someone in your church is willing to act as parish photographer, get them to contact the newspaper's picture editor sometime for a good chat on exactly what is needed, and to study the newspaper to see what sort of photographs are preferred. Of course, there are cameras and cameras, but nowadays good automatic focus cameras using 35mm film, 100ASA, 200ASA or 400ASA with automatic exposure control can achieve very acceptable results. But beware: very fast film produces grainy pictures.

- Know the deadline date for photographs, and GET THEM THERE in time. Include appropriate captions and make sure people in the photograph are correctly identified. Never write on the back of a photograph except with a chinagraph pencil. Instead, type the caption onto an A4 sheet, and paste the photograph onto the sheet with cow gum – but be careful, a good photograph strikes the picture editor, it doesn't stick to him.

PICTURE EDITOR

ORGANISATIONS

Administry
69 Sandridge Road, St Albans, Hertfordshire AL1 4AG   01727 856370

Baptist Union of Great Britain Communications Department
Baptist House, PO Box 44, 129 Broadway, Didcot, Oxfordshire OX11 8RT   01235 512077

Christian Bookstall Managers' Association
17 Rowan Walk, Crawley Down, West Sussex RH10 4JP   01342 715889

Christian Publicity Organisation
Garcia Estate, Canterbury Road, Worthing, West Sussex, BN13 1BW   01903 264556

Church of England's Communications Unit
Church House, Great Smith Street, London SW1P 3NZ   0171 222 9011

Churches Advisory Council for Local Broadcasting
PO Box 124, Westcliff-on-Sea, Essex, SS0 0QU   01702 348369

Evangelical Alliance
Communications Department, Whitefield House,
186 Kennington Park Road, London SE11 4BT   0171 582 0228

Methodist Press Office
1 Central Buildings, Westminster, London SW1H 9NH   0171 222 8010

Roman Catholic Media Office
39 Eccleston Square, London SW1V 1PD   0171 630 8220

BOOKS AVAILABLE

An Introduction to Church Communication by Richard Thomas – Lynx Communications

How to Produce a Church Magazine by John Cole – Palm Tree

Instant Art Books – Palm Tree

Keep in Touch A practical guide to help churches improve their communications
by Peter Crumpler – Scripture Union

Making Contact by Rob Marshall – Bible Society

Message on a Shoestring, a publicity handbook by Chris Radley – Marc Europe

Working with the Media by Andy Radford – Church House Communications Unit